GREAT EXPLORATIONS

SIR ERNEST SHACKLETON

By Endurance We Conquer

PATRICIA CALVERT

BENCHMARK BOOKS

MARSHALL CAVENDISH
NEW YORK

In loving memory of my husband,
George J. Calvert,
and to family and friends who helped me through his unexpected death.

Benchmark Books
99 White Plains Road
Tarrytown, NY 10591-9001
www.marshallcavendish.com

Library of Congress Cataloging-in-Publication Data
Calvert, Patricia.
Sir Ernest Shackleton: by endurance we conquer / by Patricia Calvert.
p. cm.-(Great explorations)
ISBN 0-7614-1485-1
Summary: Presents the life and Arctic explorations of Sir Ernest Shackleton.
Includes bibliographical references and index.
1. Shackleton, Ernest Henry, Sir,
1874-1922-Journeys-Antarctica-Juvenile literature. 2. Endurance (Ship) -Juvenile literature. 3. Imperial Trans-Antarctic Expedition (1914-1917) -Juvenile literature. 4. Antarctica-Discovery and exploration-Juvenile literature.
5. Imperial Trans-Antarctic Expedition (1914-1917) [I. Shackleton, Ernest Henry, Sir, 1874-1922. 2. Explorers. 3. Endurance (Ship) 4. Antarctica-Discovery and exploration.] I. Title. II. Series.
G8501914.S53C362002
2002003784

Photo Research by Candlepants Incorporated

Cover Photo: Corbis
Cover Inset: Corbis/Hulton-Deutsch Collection
The photographs in this book are used by permission and through the courtesy of: *Corbis*:
Hulton-Deutsch Collection, 5, 24, 36, 42, 44, 50, 69; Bettmann, 11, 16, 20, 25, 27, 31, 34, 41, 49, 54; Sean Sexton Collection, 14; Peter Johnson, 19; Galen Rowell, 21; Morton Beebe, 38; 47, 53, 61. *The New York Public Library, General Research Division, Astor, Lenox & Tilden Foundations*: 7, 9,10. *Scott Polar Research Institute, University of Cambridge*: 18, 22, 43, 65. *Royal Geographic Society, London*: 58.

Printed in Hong Kong

1 3 5 6 4 2

Contents

foreword

One hundred sixty million years ago, the frozen continent of Antarctica was part of a much larger landmass that included South America, South Africa, and Australia. Fossil evidence indicates that it was a semitropical region, covered with ferns, grasses, and trees, and its inhabitants were snails, beetles, reptiles, and large, flightless birds.

But when the landmass broke apart, one of the sections—5.5 million square miles (14.2 square kilometers) in size, or equivalent to the United States and Mexico combined—drifted south. It became the world's fifth-largest continent, a continent whose primary geographic feature was an enormous ice sheet, 6,500 to 12,000 feet (1,981 to 3,658 meters) thick, covering 95 percent of its surface, with snowfall measuring only two inches per year. The once-tropical region became a frozen desert, as dry as the Sahara.

Between 1800 and 1900, fifty-six expeditions deep into the southern

The doomed ship, Endurance, by the light of a full moon.

seas were recorded: twenty-five British, nineteen America, four German, and one each from Russia, Belgium, France, Australia, and Argentina. In 1819, Czar Alexander of Russia sent an expedition to the Antarctic, and in 1823 Britain dispatched a retired Royal Navy man, James Weddell, to the region. Weddell was named in his honor. In February 1821, American whalers became the first men to actually set foot in the Antarctic, and their captain, John Davis, correctly remarked, "I think this Southern land to be a continent." In 1836, the U.S. Congress approved funds for further exploration at the South Pole.

In 1890, the headstrong sixteen-year-old son of a London physician declared that he didn't intend to follow his father into medicine. Instead, he joined the British merchant marine. Ten years later, having traveled several times around the world, young Ernest Shackleton—who still had an appetite for adventure—learned that the Royal Geographical Society was planning an expedition to claim the South Pole for Britain. He volunteered to become a member of the team that was being assembled. The rest, as they say, is history, and one of the most harrowing chapters of human suffering and endurance ever documented.

ONE

A Pig-Headed, Obstinate Boy

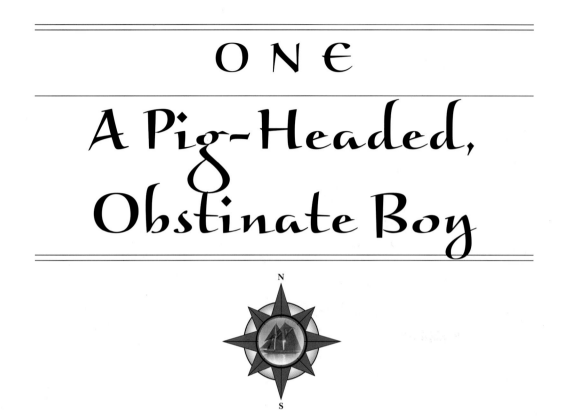

The Shackletons took their name from the village of Shackleton in Yorkshire, England. Later, several members of the family emigrated to county Kildare, Ireland, and their motto, *Fortitudinis vincimus*—"By endurance we conquer"—became a touchstone for Ernest Shackleton, their most famous descendant.

In 1872, after graduating from Trinity College, Ernest's father, Henry, settled with his new wife on a farm near the village of Kilkea, 30 miles (48.3 kilometers) from Dublin.

Ernest Henry was born on February 15, 1874, the second child and oldest son in a brood that eventually numbered ten—two boys and eight girls. Ernest's grandmother and aunts often pitched in to help with the children. Surrounded by a gaggle of women, Ernest might have become a sissy, but he was always a boy's boy. Just the same, he absorbed so many of his caretakers' tender

Ernest Henry Shackleton, after he enrolled in Dulwich College in 1887. Because he'd spent his early childhood in Ireland and spoke with an Irish accent, he was conscious of being an outsider.

qualities that years later a friend called him "a Viking with a mother's heart."

When Ernest was ten, his father moved the family to England and established a medical practice in Sydenham, a suburb of London. The Shackleton children, who had been educated at home, started public school for the first time. At Fir Lodge Preparatory School, Ernest's accent identified him as Irish, marking him as an outsider. It was a label that would haunt him the rest of his life, yet a fellow student recalled that he was "always friendly and good natured."

In 1887, at age thirteen, Ernest was enrolled in Dulwich College, a boys' school. He was regarded as an "odd boy who, in spite of an adventurous nature . . . loved a book better than a bat, solitude better than a crowd." Teachers also noted that he was a "determined, headstrong fellow." Years later, when his name became known around the world, one of them admitted, "We never discovered you when you were at Dulwich." Ernest agreed, then added, "I had not then discovered myself."

In 1890, when Ernest finished the spring term at Dulwich, he announced that he intended to go to sea. Dr. Shackleton was disappointed; he'd hoped his older son would follow him into medicine. Nevertheless, a cousin, the Reverend G. W. Woosnam, superintendent of the Mersey Mission to Seamen, arranged for the North-Western Shipping Company to take the boy as an apprentice aboard a merchant ship bound for South America.

On April 19, 1890, sixteen-year-old Ernest headed for Liverpool and signed on with the *Hoghton Tower*. He was seasick for three days, and no sooner had he recovered than he was put to work learning the ropes—literally.

Apprentices aboard the 1,700-ton (1,543-metric ton), square-rigged *Hoghton* had to memorize the names and uses of more than two hundred ropes that operated the ship's sails. Ernest also swabbed decks, loaded and unloaded cargo, and polished brass fixtures. Since storms at sea were sudden and violent, boys like himself were sometimes lashed in place on deck to keep them from being washed overboard.

The ship's crew were tough, experienced seamen who drank, cursed, and gambled—habits unknown in the genteel Shackleton household Ernest came from. The boy wrote of seeing a man "stab another with a knife in the thigh right up to the handle," and discovered that another had gone to sea to escape a murder charge. Ernest summed up his new life in a letter to a chum at Dulwich: "it is pretty hard work . . . a queer life, and a risky one."

Just as when he'd been sent off to public school, his new companions were a reminder to Ernest that he was an outsider. Again, he found solace in books, which produced an unexpected result. "The first night I took out my Bible to read they all stopped talking and laughing." Ernest wrote home, "and now every one of them reads theirs."

The *Hoghton*'s route took her around Cape Horn, the southernmost tip of the South American continent. The weather in that part of the world was unpredictable, the seas were treacherous, and generations of sailors had

Shackleton, age sixteen, in his first uniform.

9

dreaded the passage. Yet when Ernest Shackleton rounded the Cape for the first time, he said he felt "strangely drawn towards the mysterious south."

When Ernest's first apprenticeship was finished, on April 22, 1891, the captain of the *Hoghton Tower* sought out the Reverend Woosnam. He reported that Ernest was "the most pig-headed, obstinate boy I have ever come across." Yet the captain had no complaints about the boy's work, and took him on for another year.

In October 1894, at age twenty, Ernest took the Board of Trade examination and became a second mate. Four years later, he earned a master's certificate, which qualified him to be the captain of a British merchant ship anywhere in the world. Ernest now had a special reason for wanting to advance his career as quickly as possible. On one of his visits home, his sister Kathleen had introduced him to her friend Emily Dorman.

The HOUGHTON TOWER

Sir Ernest and
Lady Shackleton, 1910.

Emily, a tall, handsome woman six years older than Ernest, came from a well-to-do family and had many eligible suitors. Ernest discovered that she shared his love of Browning's poetry, but there wasn't time for them to become better acquainted before he left aboard the *Flintshire*, destined for the ports of Singapore, Nagasaki, and Yokohama.

When he returned to England, the couple exchanged copies of Browning, and Ernest decided that Emily was the woman he wanted to marry. Yet he was only a merchant seaman. He knew that his prospects must improve before he dared ask Emily's father for her hand. In 1899, when he was twenty-five, he joined the Union Castle Line, England's most prestigious shipping firm, hoping to upgrade his standing as a suitor.

He was appointed an officer on the *Tintagel Castle*, a ship carrying 1,200 British troops to fight in the Boer War in South Africa. After a second voyage, in March 1900, Ernest collaborated with the ship's surgeon, Dr. W. McLean, on a book about their experiences, *O.H.M.S.:*

An Illustrated Record of the Voyage of S.S. "Tintagel Castle." Ernest boldly invited the most famous British author of the day, Rudyard Kipling, to write an introductory poem for it. Kipling agreed, and Shackleton ordered two specially bound copies—one for Queen Victoria, the other for Emily Dorman.

When Ernest was elected a fellow of the Royal Geographical Society, he became intrigued by the society's plans for promoting Antarctic exploration. On September 13, 1900, he inquired as to whether such an expedition might have a place for him. Perhaps he recalled how much he'd enjoyed reading about the adventures of Pizarro and Livingstone, men who had explored unknown regions of the world. He might have felt like an outsider, but in his heart, Ernest Shackleton was convinced that a special destiny awaited him, too.

TWO

Afraid of Nothing

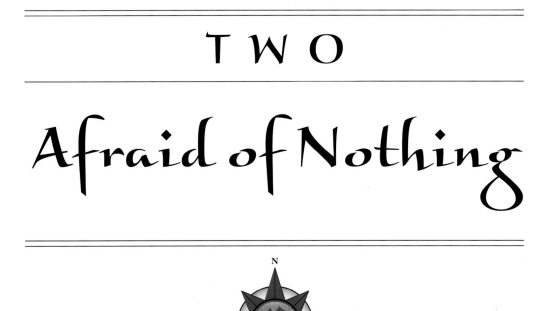

In November 1893, Sir John Murray, a British oceanographer, lectured on "The Renewal of Antarctic Exploration" at a meeting of the Royal Geographical Society in London. The aim of a new British polar expedition, Murray explained to his audience, would be to study the oceans at the bottom of the world, and to claim the South Pole as a first for England.

"Is the last great piece of maritime exploration on the surface of our Earth to be undertaken by Britons," Murray asked, "or is it to be left to those who may be destined to succeed or supplant us on the Ocean?" Shackleton couldn't put Murray's question out of his mind.

Antarctic exploration attracted Shackleton for its own sake, but he was also mindful that being included in such a venture would impress Emily's father. Ernest had already asked Mr. Dorman for her hand, admitting that marriage would have to wait until "I have . . .

Ernest Shackleton, in a formal portrait made in Ireland. In photographs, he usually wore a stern, unsmiling expression, but he was remembered by his men as a cheerful fellow who enjoyed a good laugh and played practical jokes.

THE RACE BEGINS

As the century turned, Britain wasn't the only nation interested in exploring Antarctica. In 1899, a Belgian ship commanded by Adrien de Gerlache had been trapped by ice at the bottom of the world for almost a year and survived. Norway's Carsten Borchgrevink had already established a farthest-south dogsledge record of 78°. Germany's Erich von Drygalski and Sweden's Otto Nordenskjold were planning expeditions. Clearly, a race for the South Pole was on.

position and money." He hoped that polar exploration would give him both.

For twenty years, Sir Clements Markham, president of the Royal Geographical Society, had been a champion of such exploration. Now, he pushed the National Antarctic Expedition forward by gathering donations from wealthy Englishmen, and the Prince of Wales (soon to be King Edward VII) provided a grant for the project. The *Discovery*, a coal-fired, wooden steamship fitted with sails to conserve fuel, was especially built to handle the Antarctic ice. Robert F. Scott, a thirty-two-year-old lieutenant in the Royal Navy, was named commander of the expedition. The London *Times* praised the choice, declaring, "youth is essential" for such ventures.

Ernest Shackleton submitted his application to be included on the expedition, but was turned down. A less determined man might have accepted the rejection. Not Shackleton. Instead, the stubbornness witnessed by the captain of the *Hoghton* during the boy's first apprenticeship quickly surfaced.

Shackleton energetically pressed his case. He'd made several friends in the Royal Geographical Society, among them Cedric Longstaff, whose wealthy father had contributed generously to the expedition's fund. Ernest asked the elder Longstaff to appeal to Sir Clements Markham on his behalf. After meeting Shackleton in person, Markham declared that the expedition was "fortunate in finding such an excellent . . . officer as Ernest Shackleton," and called him a "marvel of intelligent energy."

The DISCOVERY, on which Robert F. Scott made his first voyage to the Antarctic in 1901.

The other navy men selected for the expedition had been trained on steamships. Shackleton's long experience with sail was considered highly important. When his name appeared on the "Final List of Officers and Crew," it was noted that he also would be in charge of the expedition's seawater analyses.

Shackleton's first meeting with his future commander took place in the headquarters of the National Antarctic Expedition. Robert Scott and Ernest Shackleton were similar in one important respect: Both had struggled hard to achieve professional advancement, yet each had private doubts about his ability to get on in his career. They were unalike in that Scott was aloof, while Shackleton made friends easily. Their similarities and differences would later make for a difficult relationship.

On July 31, 1901, the *Discovery*, with thirty-eight men aboard, made its way down the river Thames. Emily Dorman waved good-bye from the dock, as did three of Ernest's sisters. At Cowes, the expedition's patron, now King Edward VII, came aboard with Queen Alexandra. Edward delivered a farewell speech, and then, on August 6, the ship put out to sea. Shackleton left with a high heart, for in response to his request for Emily's hand, her father had replied that his "consent to your union will not be wanting."

The special training that Shackleton needed to perform seawater analyses was provided by Dr. Hugh Robert Mill, a Scottish oceanographer who accompanied the *Discovery* as far as Spain. Mill was delighted by the young officer's "inexhaustible good humour," and noted that Shackleton "differed . . . in trend of mind from the other splendid fellows" who were on the expedition. By the time Mills left the ship in August, he and Shackleton had built a friendship that was to last the rest of their lives. The crew also took a liking to Shackleton, who "was always ready to have a yarn with us."

One of the most important onboard friendships Shackleton made was with Frank Wild, a schoolmaster's son. Wild had gone to sea after

The crew of the DISCOVERY. Shackleton is fifth from the left. On his right is Dr. Edward Wilson, and in the center with his long captain's coat, is Robert F. Scott. The three men were members of the team that made the Southern Journey, but were unable to reach the South Pole.

realizing the classroom was too tame for him. He was warmhearted, and he had an appetite for adventure—a man after Shackleton's own heart. In January 1902, Scott established a base camp in Antarctica at McMurdo Sound, a bay in the southwest corner of the Ross Sea. The bay was thirty-five miles across, and sheltered by slopes on both sides. In the distance, two distinctive landmarks, Mount Erebus and Mount Terror—volcanoes—rose out of the rough, icy terrain.

Part of the expedition's diet was provided by forty-five sheep that were driven on board by admiring New Zealand farmers at Lyttleton House on Christmas Eve. When the ship reached the Antarctic ice, the

The Ross Ice Shelf, also called the Great Ice Barrier, was named for British naval officer James Clark Ross, who located it in 1841. It rises like a dazzling white wall two hundred feet out of the ocean. Ross also was the first to locate the South Magnetic Pole.

animals were slaughtered, and their carcasses hung in the rigging of the *Discovery*. The meat froze solid, which preserved it for later use. Scott believed that a feast of roast mutton every Sunday, a familiar English custom, would boost the spirits of the crew during the long winter ahead.

Scott had admired the polar work of the famous Norwegian explorer Fridtjof Nansen, who advised the use of dogs for polar travel. To most Englishmen, however, a dog was a pet, not a means of transportation. Since no member of the expedition had any experience handling sledge dogs, the dog teams and sledging parties did not perform as well as they might have. Scott decided to try manhauling—having the men pull the sledges themselves.

An Era Ends, Another Begins

The National Antarctic Expedition set out at the moment in British history when the Victorian Age came to an end. Eighty-one-year-old Queen Victoria, England's ruler for almost sixty-four years, died on January 22, 1901. The "longest and most prosperous reign on record" was over, and the world was changing rapidly. The Boer War in South Africa, the rise of Germany as an industrial power, and increasing competition from the United States had put England on its toes. The nation was as ready to welcome a polar hero as Shackleton was eager to become one.

Queen Victoria came to the British throne in 1837, at age eighteen. She ruled until her death in 1901, more than sixty-three years later. She had vowed as a girl, "I will be good," and was deeply loved by her subjects.

Afraid of Nothing

On February 19, 1902, Shackleton set out on a three-day sledge expedition to explore nearby White Island. He was accompanied by Dr. Edward Wilson, the expedition's junior surgeon, and Hartley Ferrar, a geologist. The three men discovered firsthand the backbreaking effort required to drag heavy sledges across almost impassable terrain. *Sastrugi*, wavelike formations created in the snow by the ceaseless action of the wind, were among the party's greatest obstacles.

A second foray, which started across the ice on March 4, ended tragically. During a driving snowstorm, one of the sailors tumbled over an icy cliff and plunged to his death. A second sailor, eighteen-year-old Charles Hare, seemed to have met the same fate. To everyone's amazement, however, Hare made his way back to the *Discovery* on March 13, having survived by being buried in the snow, which kept him from freezing to death.

Shackleton soon added the editing of a shipboard newspaper to his many chores. Dr. Wilson turned out to be a fine illustrator, and the first issue of the *South Polar Times* appeared in April 1902. Albert

---

SASTRUGI, carved in the snow by the prevailing winds, made any travel exhausting and time-consuming for both men and sledge dogs.

Ernest Shackleton (left), Commander Robert Scott (middle), and Edward Wilson (right) were in high spirits as they prepared to set off for the South Pole in November 1902.

Armitage, the second in command of the expedition wrote that the ambition of the paper was to combine "the best qualities of all the penny and halfpenny London dailies." It even included comics!

On June 12, 1902, Commander Scott spoke privately to Dr. Wilson about an official "Southern Journey" sledge party, whose purpose would be to claim the South Pole for Britain. He hadn't decided whether it should consist of two or three men, but made it clear that he wanted Wilson to be one of them. For safety's sake, Wilson advised Scott, it would be wise to make it a party of three. Who should be the third? Scott asked. Shackleton was the man Wilson had in mind, and he was precisely who Scott himself was considering.

Shackleton didn't belong to the regular navy, as did Scott and Wilson, yet his "striking personality, admirable humour, and inexhaustible energy" made him an attractive choice. Thus Ernest Shackleton, twenty-eight years old, began his quest for the South Pole. He couldn't have guessed that the frozen, forbidding Antarctic would hold him in its thrall until the very day of his death.

THREE

Don't Expect a Feather Bed

On October 1, 1902, Scott, Shackleton, and Michael Barnes left the base camp at McMurdo Sound to bury six weeks' supply of food in the snow along the route that the expedition planned to follow southward. Such depots, established at regular intervals, meant the sledges wouldn't have to be loaded as heavily during the actual push for the Pole—1,600 miles (2,575 kilometers) inland—which was scheduled to begin two weeks later.

But when the ship's doctor, Dr. Koettliz, examined the crew, he discovered that nearly all the men were suffering from scurvy. The expedition was delayed so that Scott could put everyone on a diet of fresh seal meat, vegetables, and canned fruit to counteract the disease. The condition of all but two of the men—Shackleton and Scott himself—improved rapidly. Shackleton struck a realistic note in his diary: "danger is rife . . . it is all part of the game . . . we did not expect a feather bed down here."

When Scott decided it was safe to proceed with the expedition, he sent

Ernest Shackleton, 1908.

a support party of twelve men ahead to break a trail and establish additional supply depots. Three days later—on Sunday, November 2, 1902—he, Shackleton, and Wilson followed with five sledges and nineteen dogs.

Leaving the safety of the base camp unsettled Wilson, who fondly called his cabin aboard the ship "a small sanctuary for happy recollections, lamp soot, and general comfort." He realized that for the next three months, he and his companions would face "the absolutely unknown South." Even Shackleton, usually so high-spirited, admitted in a letter to Emily, "I believe in God . . . [and] have tried to do my best as a man, the rest I leave to Him."

As planned, the support party turned back to base camp. Half the men left on November 13, and the remainder left on November 15. The three explorers were on their own. Temperatures rose to over 20 degrees Fahrenheit (over –7 degrees Celsius), softening the snow to mush. Travel became arduous, because the sledges were loaded with a ton and a half of supplies—the original load, plus what had been left behind by the support team. This meant that each dog needed to pull about 150 pounds (68 kilograms), or twice what experienced dog drivers would have expected of them. As a result, the dogs quickly wore themselves out. By comparison, Otto Nordenskjold boasted in his book, *Antarctic*, published in 1904, that "we had immense help from our dogs," because he knew what their limits were. To complicate matters further, the British explorers, unlike the Norwegians, had never used skis before, and they wasted precious energy trying to learn on the job.

Men and dogs struggled gallantly against the poor conditions, yet averaged only about 4 or 5 miles (6 or 8 kilometers) a day. It became clear there wouldn't be any dramatic dash to the Pole, as Scott had hoped. Health became an issue, as well. All three men caught colds, and Shackleton developed a nagging cough. Yet the eerie beauty of a landscape where sea, sky, and snow seemed to merge, fascinated him: " . . . slowly but surely we are finding out the secret of this wonderful place," he observed in his diary.

THE SCOURGE OF SCURVY

The ravages of scurvy were first described by the Greek physician Hippocrates (?460-377 BC), who observed its effects among soldiers, sailors, and prisoners who were deprived proper diets. When Robert Falcon Scott's expedition set its sights on the South Pole, the "Black Death of the sea" (also called scorbutum, scururie, scirvie, scurby, or skryby), was blamed on the poisonous effects of eating canned or salted meat. As early as the thirteenth century, however, seamen realized it could be prevented by eating a diet rich in fruits and vegetables. In 1776, the British explorer, Captain James Cook, discovered on his fist voyage that vitamin C-rich Kerguelen cabbage—a plant native to the Kerguelen Islands—helped counteract the disease. Scurvy wasn't merely an inconvenience—it was a killer. Early symptoms included bleeding gums, inflamed eyes, stiff joints, muscle pain, and swollen legs. Untreated individuals became delirious, lapsed into a coma, and died. Scurvy afflicted 23,000 French troops during the Crimean War, and 15 percent of America's Civil War casualties were attributed to the disease.

In 1753, a Scottish physician, James Lind, published A TREATISE ON SCURVY, proving that the disease—which killed more British sailors than combat—was caused by a dietary deficiency of vitamin C. He recommended that lemons, oranges, and limes—all rich in vitamin C—be added to the diet of seamen. As a result, British sailors were nicknamed limeys.

Robert f. Scott checks his sled dogs at base camp before setting out on his expedition to the South Pole.

Constant hunger soon made "this wonderful place" less than wonderful. Scott had unwisely permitted an unlimited consumption of food, only to realize after a month on the trail that supplies wouldn't hold out. Meals were cut from three per day to two, adding to the decline in the explorers' energy.

Scott had picked Shackleton for the journey partly because of his good humor, but Scott himself could be short-tempered. Worse, sometimes he was verbally abusive. When Shackleton accidentally knocked over a cooking pot, Scott flew into a rage, threatening to abandon the journey then and there. Wilson, acting as a mediator, calmed him down and pointed out that public opinion would be highly negative if he quit over such a trivial matter.

On December 9, only five weeks after the party left McMurdo Sound, a sledge dog named Snatcher died. Shackleton was given the grisly task of skinning and butchering it, then feeding the meat to Snatcher's teammates. One by one, as each dog became weaker, it was killed and fed to its companions. The loss of each animal meant the men had to do more of the hauling themselves, even though their diet of hoosh—a concoction of pemmican (dried meat mixed with fat, cooked in water, then eaten as a stew)—was completely lacking in vitamin C, which would have prevented scurvy.

Christmas Day, 1902, blazed with sunshine, and the expedition made its best progress yet—10 miles (16 kilometers). However, Shackleton admitted gloomily, "Medical examtn. Shews Capt [Scott] & I to be inclined to scurvy . . . [but] we hope to cross 82° S. in 2 days." That goal—82° South latitude—lured them on, for it meant they would have bested Borchgrevink's record of 78° 50' South latitude, set in 1900.

On December 28, after making camp, Scott decided to leave the sledges behind and press forward on skis. By New Year's Eve, however, bad weather had forced the trio back, 460 miles (740 kilometers) from their goal. Food supplies were dangerously low. Dogs continued to die—"Clarence gave up the ghost," Shackleton wrote about the latest canine victim in his diary—and when Spud became too weak to keep up, he was loaded onto a sledge, only to be killed later the same day.

By the second week of January 1903, the exhausted explorers were on the verge of collapse. The two dogs remaining of the original nineteen had to be killed, and when Scott examined Shackleton's gums again, he found them more inflamed than before. More ominously, Shackleton was coughing up blood, a sign that his scurvy was progressing to a critical level.

Shackleton's condition worsened. He hemorrhaged on January 15, and Scott and Wilson believed he wouldn't live through the night. Shackleton was devastated. He'd always been proud of his strength and stamina, but now he was laid so low that Scott ordered him to ride on one of the sledges and be hauled along like a dying dog. Nothing could have been more humiliating. Yet Shackleton mentioned his illness only briefly in his diary. Half-jokingly, he predicted that he'd outlive Scott and Wilson. He was right.

On February 3, 1903, when the trio was 6 miles (9.65 kilometers) from McMurdo Sound, they were greeted by two members from base camp. Bernacchi remembered that the explorers' "swollen lips & peeled complexions, & bloodshot eyes . . . made them almost unrecognizable . . . [and] Shackleton seemed very ill indeed."

Cheers, songs, and toasts awaited the men when they got to camp, but Shackleton confessed that he "wasn't up to the mark." Instead of joining the celebration, he took a bath—his first in ninety-four days—and crawled into bed. A few days later, on February 15, he celebrated his twenty-ninth birthday.

A Norwegian whaling ship, the *Morning*, had arrived at McMurdo Sound with fresh supplies. Commander Scott now had to decide whether or not to remain in the southern seas for a second year and make another try for the Pole. Immediately, a controversy arose over whether Shackleton's poor health would allow him to continue.

On March 1, 1903, Shackleton was dismissed from the expedition. He left the *Discovery* and trekked 4 miles (64 kilometers) across the ice to where the *Morning* lay at anchor in a patch of open water. It was a beautiful day, he recalled, "but a sad one indeed for me . . . I cannot write much about it, but it touched me more than I can say when the men . . . gave me 3 parting cheers." Once, he'd said that he didn't expect a feather bed at the bottom of the world; he couldn't have foreseen that he'd be sent home early, like a schoolboy with a bad case of sniffles.

FOUR

No Eagles in the Barnyard

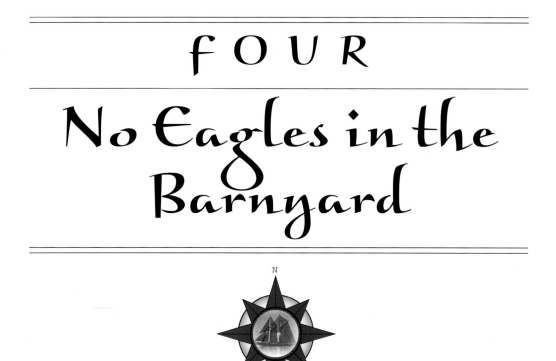

On June 2, 1903, Ernest Shackleton arrived in England. No noisy fanfare greeted his return, as he'd once dreamed. Instead, he found himself in the middle of a hot dispute brewing among the backers of the National Antarctic Expedition.

Commander Scott was being roundly criticized for allowing the *Discovery* to become locked in the ice, then deciding to stay for a second year in Antarctica, but others just as vigorously supported his actions. Shackleton, the only man with any on-the-spot information, was caught in the cross fire between critics and champions of the expedition and its leader. It is a measure of Shackleton's character, that although he believed he'd been sent home unjustly, he never stooped to criticize Scott; nor did he take sides in the debate.

In July 1903, with the support of the sponsors of the National Antarctic Expedition, Shackleton applied to the Royal Navy for an appointment as a lieutenant. He hoped that a naval commission would help him qualify as a member of future expeditions. The officers' lists were full, however, and he had to be content with admission to the reserves.

Shackleton might not have been greeted as a hero on his return from Antarctica, but soon he began to enjoy a certain kind of fame. He was a skilled storyteller, and the public was eager to hear what he had to say about a part of the world that few people knew anything about. Then, although he had no professional journalistic experience, he was hired as an editor of the *Royal Magazine*. "There was something about him that compelled confidence," another editor remembered. "He was the most friendly hail-fellow-well-met man I have ever come across."

In November 1903, Shackleton was invited to lecture at the prestigious Royal Scottish Geographical Society in Edinburgh. Two months

Ernest Shackleton received recognition from many admirers after his return from the Scott expedition. Here, photographed many years later, he is shown (left) being presented with a bouquet of heather.

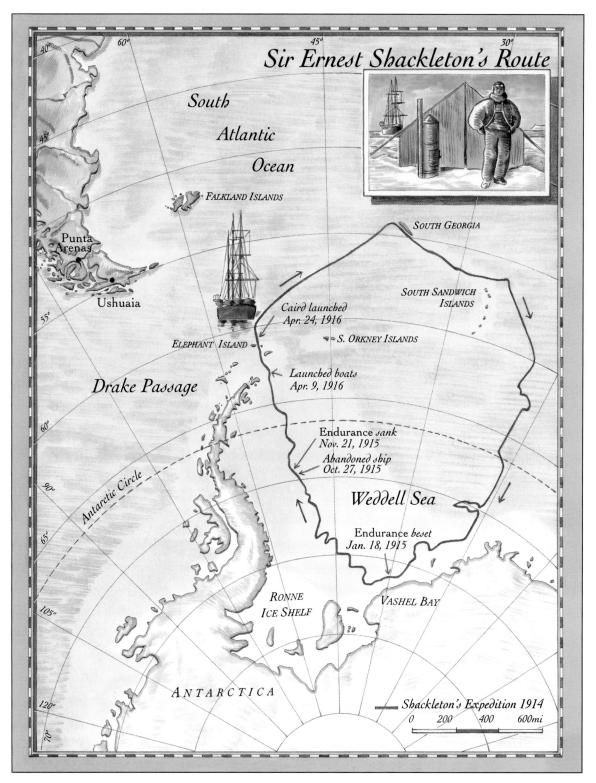

Sir Ernest Shackleton's Route

South

Atlantic

Ocean

FALKLAND ISLANDS

SOUTH GEORGIA

Punta
Arenas

SOUTH SANDWICH
ISLANDS

Caird launched
Apr. 24, 1916

S. ORKNEY ISLANDS

Ushuaia

ELEPHANT ISLAND

Drake Passage

Launched boats
Apr. 9, 1916

Endurance *sank*
Nov. 21, 1915

Antarctic Circle

Abandoned ship
Oct. 27, 1915

Weddell Sea

Endurance *beset*
Jan. 18, 1915

RONNE
ICE SHELF

VASHEL BAY

A N T A R C T I C A

Shackleton's Expedition 1914

0   200   400   600mi

later, he was asked to become the secretary of the organization, and he announced that his first goal would be to improve the quality of the society's guest speakers. Under his leadership, attendance grew from 250 to more than 1,630, and the society's membership increased from 1,430 to 1,832.

In spite of his disappointments, an exciting new life had opened for Shackleton, and yet another chapter awaited him. On April 9, 1904, he married Emily Dorman, and the couple moved into their first home, at 14 South Learmonth Gardens in Edinburgh. The social climate of the city—usually frosty to newcomers—quickly warmed to the young couple, for Emily proved to be as charming as her husband. The newlyweds were accepted by people and enjoyed dinner parties, luncheons, and golf—at which Emily was said to be much better than her husband!

In September 1904, when the *Discovery* returned to England after its second year in the Antarctic, having failed again to reach the Pole, it was Scott who became the center of public attention. Suddenly, Shackleton felt like a nobody; it was a bitter reminder of his lifelong status as an outsider. However, even though he hadn't participated in the second year of the expedition, he received the king's Polar Medal, along with his former companions.

When Scott and Shackleton met again, each avoided mentioning the difficulties of their former relationship. On the contrary, Shackleton—who was naturally warmhearted—generously invited Scott to speak in Edinburgh. "It will be a great thing for the Society if you can come up," he said.

Scott gave his first lecture in November 1904, not realizing what a successful speaker Shackleton had become. Scott tended to be stiff and formal, and talked down to his audience, whereas Shackleton, with his common touch, was able to create a warm, dynamic relationship with any roomful of listeners. As F. W. Everett, editor of the *Royal Magazine* noted, Shackleton "had the true sailor's love for spinning a yarn . . . he

A feud at the Opposite Pole

Polar explorers could be notoriously thin-skinned. Robert E. Peary prepared for his fifth assault on the North Pole, at the opposite end of the earth, in 1898. But he soon discovered that a Norwegian explorer, Otto Sverdrup, planned a similar venture. Peary denounced it as "an unprincipled attempt" to capitalize on his—Peary's—earlier achievements. In October, when Peary accidentally stumbled upon Sverdrup's camp, the Norwegian invited him to enjoy a cup of coffee. Peary haughtily refused, causing many to accuse the American of poor sportsmanship.

American explorer Robert E. Peary, September 1909. Peary announced—after eight attempts over more than twenty years—that he'd finally reached the North Pole. A fellow American, Dr. Frederick Cook, also claimed to have reached the Pole. An investigation by members of the U.S. Congress judged Peary's claims to be valid.

made us see the things he spoke of, and held us all spell-bound." Scott didn't possess the same skills.

Although the two men refrained from speaking about the events in Antarctica, when Scott published *The Voyage of the Discovery*, he pointedly revealed details of the first expedition that were painful for Shackleton. "Our invalid was so exhausted that . . . we carried him," he wrote, then referred to Shackleton with phrases that would have shamed the least egotistical of men.

Shackleton's success as a speaker inspired friends to urge him to run for Parliament. He agreed, but when the decision caused dissension among members of the Royal Geographical Society, he resigned his secretarial post before campaigning for office. Shackleton was an adventurer, however, not a politician, and lost the election on January 16, 1905. "I got all the applause and the other fellows got all the votes," he joked. Winston Churchill, the future prime minister of England, also was a candidate; he won his seat.

Shackleton made light of his loss, yet the rejection angered him. Deep down, he couldn't forget the embarrassment he'd suffered in Antarctica. Only one thing—a successful return to the frozen South, the scene of his humiliation—would heal his wounded pride. Not even the birth of his first son, Raymond, on February 2, 1905, was enough to soothe his spirit.

In August 1905, the Norwegian explorer Roald Amundsen navigated his ship, the *Gjoa*, through the Northwest Passage, which connected the Atlantic and Pacific Oceans. The feat was regarded as a major geographical accomplishment. Such news heightened Shackleton's eagerness to enter what was becoming an explorer's sweepstakes.

On December 23, 1906, Emily gave birth to a daughter, Cecily. Although Shackleton's wife longed for a tranquil home, she knew her husband well enough to say many years later, "One must not chain down an eagle in a barnyard." She knew better than anyone that her husband was not destined to live an ordinary life. He had always believed a special destiny awaited him, and only a return to Antarctica would satisfy his dream. On February 11, 1907, Shackleton hurried to the office of the Royal Geographical Society, where he intended to ask for backing for a venture that he called the British Antarctic Expedition. He was startled to find two visitors there: Roald Amundsen and Fridtjof Nansen, among the most experienced polar explorers of the day. He didn't let their presence prevent him from making his request, but he was disappointed by the cool reception he got from the society, and he left empty-handed.

The famous Norwegians weren't the only ones planning polar forays. Dr. Jean-Baptiste Charcot of France intended to make an assault on the South Pole by balloon and motorized sledge. Henryk Arctowski of Poland, a friend of Amundsen's, had gotten backing from Belgium for an expedition. An American, Dr. Frederick Cook, had published an article about how he planned to reach the Pole. The competition to be first to get to the bottom of the world was hotter than ever.

Undaunted by rumors of competition, Shackleton forged ahead. He remembered the approach William Spiers Bruce had used, and gathered pledges of financing from his wealthy new friends in Edinburgh. He needed a second in command, and wrote to Dr. Wilson, reminding him of the world they'd done together on the Scott expedition. "Don't say No until we have had a talk," he begged. Wilson was involved in a two-year scientific project, however, and declined to give it up. But he cautioned Shackleton that it would be unethical to use McMurdo Sound as the starting point for his own expedition.

Roald Amundsen of Norway, one of the world's most experienced polar explorers. He reached the South Pole on December 14, 1911, and attributed his success—on the first try—to the use of a completely different route that neither Scott nor Shackleton had considered. However, he generously praised Shackleton's earlier efforts.

F I V E

An Old Dog for the Hard Road

"I do wholly agree with the right lying with Scott to use the base before anyone else," Dr. Wilson warned. Otherwise, it would seem as if "you forestalled Scott who had a prior claim." Shackleton said he couldn't sleep for three nights after receiving Wilson's reply.

His next choice was George Mulock from the Royal Navy, who had been Shackleton's replacement when he was sent home from the *Discovery* expedition. Mulock also declined, explaining that he'd already volunteered to go with Scott.

Already volunteered to go with Scott . . .

Suddenly, Shackleton realized that the chilly reception he'd received in the offices of the Royal Geographical Society had nothing to do with the presence of Amundsen and Nansen. The Society had already decided to back Scott! Days later, Shackleton received two letters from Scott himself, accusing him of disloyalty for planning an expedition of his own.

The base at McMurdo Sound was *his*, Scott insisted, and nobody else's.

Shackleton knew he must organize his expedition with all possible speed. Emily—mindful of the fact that her husband had been forced to leave the Scott expedition for health reasons—persuaded him to see a doctor in London. But Shackleton, at age thirty-three, was determined to avoid a thorough examination, which might reveal more than he wanted anyone—including himself—to know. "I think he examined the specialist instead of the specialist examining him," a friend remarked.

Shackleton tried again to recruit former members of the Scott expedition. All declined. However, when news got around that he was looking for men, he received more than 400 applications. From among

Robert F. Scott's base, built in 1911.

them, he chose young amateur adventurers, for two reasons: Such men were eager to experience the thrill of polar exploration, yet they wouldn't be apt to challenge his leadership.

By May 1907, Shackleton had assembled a crew. He made it clear to all recruits that everyone would be equal. Each man, regardless of rank, would be expected to do his share of work, no matter what it turned out to be.

Fridtjof Nansen, a contender for the Pole himself, was famous for his lack of rivalry, and when Shackleton asked for advice, he gave it generously. Shackleton ignored much of it, causing Nansen to observe that he'd spent "too little time" on preparations. He predicted that Shackleton, like Scott, would face probable failure on his second journey.

Nansen had advised Shackleton to use skis; Shackleton rejected his idea. He would walk to the Pole, he declared. For pack animals, he intended to use hardy Manchurian ponies, which he believed could travel 20 to 25 miles (32 to 40 kilometers) a day. Nansen was shocked. In 1893, Robert E. Peary had tried using burros at the North Pole; they had quickly ended up as dog food. Nansen was even more amazed to hear that Shackleton intended to take an automobile to the Pole!

No sooner had Shackleton arranged to hire the *Bjorn*—a fine three-year-old, 500-ton (454 metric-tons) sealing ship built especially for working in polar ice—than some of his financial backing collapsed. The news would have drained the determination out of anyone else, but Shackleton swiftly modified his plans.

If he couldn't hire a ship like the *Bjorn*, he'd arrange for a cheaper one. The *Nimrod*, a forty-two-year-old sealer was available, but Shackleton was taken aback the first time he laid eyes on her. She was a small, grimy vessel that hardly looked up to the task expected of her—but she was all he could afford.

Rupert England, who'd been the first mate on the *Morning*, the ship that had carried Shackleton home from McMurdo Sound in 1903, was hired on as captain. John King Davis signed up as chief officer, and he never forgot his first impression of Shackleton. "There was about him the unmistakable look of a deep-sea sailor," he wrote.

On New Year's Day, 1908, the *Nimrod* left Lyttleton Harbor in New Zealand and headed south. Seven years, almost to the day, had passed since the Scott expedition had left the same harbor, on Christmas Eve, 1901.

Shackleton had promised Scott he wouldn't use McMurdo Sound as a base camp, and he picked King Edward Land for his winter quarters. However, bad weather, combined with pack ice, forced him to go back on his word. On January 29, 1908, for the safety of his crew and the *Nimrod*, Shackleton reentered McMurdo Sound. Historians who have examined his decision agree that it was born of common sense, not treachery, and that if positions had been reversed, Scott would have done the same.

Food, coal, dogs, ponies, and the automobile were taken ashore. Captain England worried that if the *Nimrod* lingered too long it would be frozen in, just as the *Discovery* had been several years earlier. He couldn't take such a risk, he said. On February 22, the *Nimrod* headed back to New Zealand, leaving the expedition on its own until the ship's scheduled return, months later.

The day after the *Nimrod* left, 129 penguins were killed and buried in the snow to serve as a future food supply. A large shelter was built on shore, including private cubicles measured 6 by 7 feet (1.8 by 2.1 meters), to be shared by two men. A barn was erected for the ponies, and a kennel built for the dogs, where two of the females gave birth to puppies.

"The presence of the dogs . . . was very cheerful," Shackleton wrote, "and gave a homelike feeling to the place." A photographic darkroom was set up, and the men conducted scientific experiments, collected samples of plant life, and measured temperature fluctuations. A

Fridtjof Nansen, a professor of zoology from Norway, and the first man to cross the Greenland ice cap, in 1888. Like his countryman, Roald Amundsen, Nansen was admired for his skill with dog sledges and skis. When Shackleton asked him for advice, Nansen gave it willingly.

makeshift surgical ward was created when nineteen-year-old Philip Brocklehurst suffered frostbite and had to have a toe amputated.

On September 19, 1908, the automobile made its first journey. To reduce its weight, Shackleton had it stripped to its chassis, the engine, and a seat for one driver. He was pleased when the vehicle ran well for 8 miles (13 kilometers), carrying 750 pounds (340 kilograms) of supplies.

"A glorious day for our start," he noted on October 29, 1908. The Pole lay 880 statute miles away (1,416 kilometers), and the plan was to cross the Great Ice Barrier, then take the straightest possible route south. A party of four—Shackleton, Eric Marshall, Jameson Adams, and Frank Wild—set out with the car, four ponies, and enough food to last for three months.

The ponies struggled valiantly over the rough terrain. The car quit. A blizzard came up, burying the tents. On November 21, hardly a month

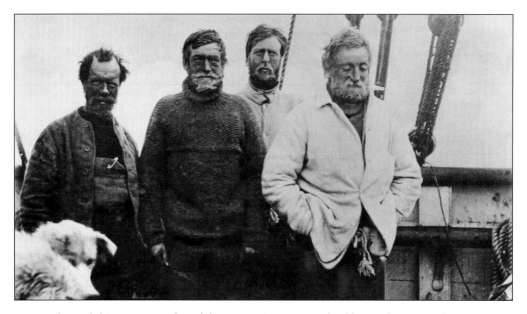

Frank Wild, Ernest Shackleton, Eric Marshall, and Jameson Adams (left to right) aboard the NIMROD, March 1909. Shackleton named his second voyage the British Antarctic Expedition, funded it with private donations, and came within 97 miles (156 kilometers) of the South Pole, setting a record for Britain.

after leaving home base, a pony named Chinaman had to be shot. A similar fate befell Grisi and Quan. "The killing of the ponies was not pleasant work," Shackleton confessed, "but we had the satisfaction of knowing the animals had been well fed and well treated up to the last." On December 7, Socks fell into a deep crevasse and couldn't be rescued.

On Christmas Day, though food was scarce, Shackleton boosted the men's morale by treating them to a sumptuous meal, complete with plum pudding. By January 9, 1909, however, the team members realized they were becoming too weak to make a final dash for the Pole. Yet they had reached a new latitude—88° South latitude only 97 miles (156 kilometers) from their longed—for prize. For all his regret about not reaching the Pole, Shackleton had "done more than anyone could have believed possible" under the circumstances. He had gotten his men back safely, and although they were "thin and worn," none showed signs of scurvy, which had plagued the Scott expedition.

Continuing the journey would have meant there wouldn't be enough food left to get all the way back to base camp. As it was, on many days the men's food allowance consisted of four biscuits, 2 ounces (57 grams)

On his second try for the South Pole, Shackleton took an Arrol-Johnston automobile with him. It had been manufactured in Paisley, Scotland, and built especially to meet the demands of polar exploration. Little was known at that time about the effects of severe cold on gasoline motors, however, and the car was abandoned after a short journey.

of cheese, and one cup of pemmican. They were forced to eat the last of the horse meat, which had spoiled, giving everyone severe diarrhea. Shackleton disguised his worry, but asked Wild to lead the men in singing "Lead Kindly Light." The hymn's most telling line, "The night is dark, and I am far from home," summed up the expedition's predicament.

The unexplained health problems that had plagued Shackleton on the Scott expedition returned to haunt him. He pushed himself hard— *too* hard, thought Wild, who noted that Shackleton did "far more than his share of work." It was as if he were determined to prove, once and for all, that he had the strength and endurance of ten men.

After the ENDURANCE was abandoned on October 27, 1915, men, dogs, and equipment were moved to a new home on an ice floe named Ocean Camp. The crew was allowed to carry only two pounds of personal possessions off the doomed ship, which went down on November 21. On January 1, 1916, they moved to a new location, Patience Camp.

At both ends of the planet, time was a ruthless dictator. Polar explorers were constantly wary of becoming locked in the ice. Therefore, Shackleton had ordered the *Nimrod* to sail for home by February 28, 1909, even if the team hadn't returned. Only 33 miles (53 kilometers) from base camp, with no time to spare, Marshall and Adams, young men in their twenties, became too weak to press on.

It was up to Shackleton and Wild to get to base camp to keep the *Nimrod* from sailing. "It's an old dog for the hard road every time," Shackleton told Wild with pride as they—both several years older than Marshall and Adams—made a dash to stop the *Nimrod*. Shackleton's expedition had made a journey of 992 miles (1,596 kilometers) in 123 days, going 366 miles (589 kilometers) farther south than any previous explorer. Best of all, they'd bested Scott's record, which was a sweet revenge for Shackleton.

On June 13, 1909, London's *Daily Mirror* praised Shackleton as "A Man Born to Rule." Everywhere he went, he was hailed as a hero, and he was knighted by King Edward. He toured Italy, Germany, Russia, and Canada, giving 123 lectures in six months. In the U.S., President Taft invited him to the White House. He wrote *The Heart of the Antarctic*, a two-volume account of his southern expedition, called the best book of its day about polar travel.

SIX

The Long Road Home

Praise for Shackleton wasn't universal, however. Robert F. Scott called his former team member "a professed liar" for going back on his pledge not to use McMurdo Sound. He vowed bitterly never to have anything to do with him again. In 1910, however, when Scott announced his plans to return to the Antarctic himself, Shackleton generously offered to help organize the supplies aboard his new ship, the *Terra Nova*.

Even as Scott was organizing his next expedition, Norway's Roald Amundsen had a keen eye trained on the South Pole. When Scott arrived in Antarctica in March 1911, he discovered that Amundsen had already established a base camp at the Bay of Whales. He realized—no doubt with a touch of panic—that he was in for a real race. When Shackleton learned of Amundsen's presence in the South, he observed that the Norwegian stood the better chance of victory, because of his long experience with dog teams and skis.

CONTROVERSY AT THE OPPOSITE POLE

Fame and wealth were bestowed on the men who discovered the frozen ends of the earth, which made it tempting for them to deceive the world about having achieved their goals. In 1909, two Americans—Robert F. Peary and Frederick A. Cook—both announced that they had reached the North Pole. After months of investigation, experts concluded that Cook had falsified his evidence. Peary was judged to be the victor. However, questions still remain about *his* claims, and the controversy permanently tarnished the glory that Peary—like Shackleton—had hoped to enjoy.

Ernest Shackleton (right) with Robert Peary, discoverer of the North Pole. The explorers had one trait in common: Each man considered himself to be an "outsider," which might have accounted for the fact that each man struggled valiantly to reach his goal—the North Pole for Peary, the South Pole for Shackleton.

It pained Shackleton to observe the explorations of others from the sidelines. Yet his own life was full, and included the birth, on July 15, 1911, of a second son, Edward Alexander (later to become Lord Shackleton). Less happily, Shackleton had an episode of illness that he dismissed as "acute rheumatism," but which medical experts now surmise was probably a mild heart attack. As always, Shackleton refused to consult a doctor, fearing what an examination might reveal. When Amundsen announced to the world that he'd reached the South Pole on December 14, 1911, Shackleton praised the achievement, noting that the Norwegian had gone by a route totally different from any that he or Scott had ever considered. Amundsen, in turn, asserted that if Shackleton himself had started from the Bay of Whales, *he* would have been the one to get to the Pole first.

The South Pole had now been reached—not once, but twice—and Shackleton admitted that "unless I can be the first to get there I have no particular desire to get there at all." Nevertheless, dreams of Antarctica still haunted him. As he confessed to an old friend, Hugh Robert Mill, "I desperately want to have one more go."

After each journey, Shackleton promised Emily it would be his last, but soon he was planning another dramatic adventure. It was true that he hadn't been the first to reach the Pole, but another first remained to be achieved: No one had ever crossed the Antarctic continent from one side to the other. Shackleton planned to cross over the Pole, starting at the Weddell Sea, then press on to the opposite coast, along the Ross Sea.

Arranging financing was always the first step in any such venture. But the same men who'd called Shackleton a hero after his second expedition suddenly became cautious about loaning him money. Shackleton stubbornly pointed out what he'd already accomplished in the Antarctic, and finally was able to wrangle enough funds to arrange for a better ship than the grimy little *Nimrod*.

Even before Shackleton's departure, polar experts expressed concern about his latest scheme. His proposed journey—1,500 miles (2,414 kilo-

TRAGEDY AT THE BOTTOM OF THE WORLD

On January 18, 1912, one month after Roald Amundsen reached the South Pole, Robert F. Scott and his four-man team arrived at the same destination. No doubt it was a stunning disappointment when they discovered that the Norwegian flag was already planted at the site they hoped to claim in England's honor. On their return trip to McMurdo Sound, two team members—Edgar Evans and Lawrence E.G. Oates—died from the combined effects of frigid temperatures and starvation. Although a cache of food was buried only 11 miles (18 kilometers) away, Edward A. Wilson, Henry B. Bowers, and Scott himself didn't have enough strength to continue after losing their companions. Scott managed to keep up his diary until the day of his death, which came on March 29. Eight months later, a search team led by British naval surgeon Dr. Edward Atkinson discovered the bodies, along with Scott's diary.

Captain Robert F. Scott's ship in the Antarctic.

meters) over terrain no man had ever set foot on—was to be completed in one hundred days, or about 15 miles (24 kilometers) per day. In spite of the fact that the area around the Weddell Sea was known for its foul weather, Shackleton had made no allowance for unexpected difficulties en route.

Yet the moment word got out that he was planning a third journey, applications came in from all over the world. Among the men Shackleton picked were Frank Wild, and Thomas Crean as second officer. Frank Worsley signed on as the ship's captain, and this time Shackleton heeded the advice of the Norwegian explorers. He would use dogs and skis.

Sir Ernest Shackleton waves from aboard the ship ENDURANCE at Millwall Docks in London, England.

On August 1, 1914, as a lone bagpiper on London's West India docks played "The Wearing o' the Green," the twenty-seven-man expedition left England. The *Polaris*, powered both by sail and coal-fired steam engines, had been built in Norway especially to withstand the assault of the ice that waited at the bottom of the world. Before embarking, however, Shackleton had renamed the ship the *Endurance*, in honor of his family's motto, "By endurance we conquer."

Three months after leaving England, the *Endurance* arrived at South Georgia, a rocky, mountainous island off the tip of South America. There, the Norwegians had established a whaling station named Grytviken. On December 5, 1914—summertime in the Antarctic, when the Weddell Sea is usually ice-free—the *Endurance* headed south.

For three days, the seas were clear. On December 8, pack ice appeared—loose, flat cakes mixed with larger pieces of iceberg. Shackleton consulted Captain Worsley, and they agreed to pursue a zigzag course toward what surely would be open water. However, they noticed that as the *Endurance* dodged the floating ice, it closed ominously behind them. Ten days later, the ice tightened further. There was nothing to do but press forward. Then, to Shackleton's great relief, open sea finally was reached.

His relief was short-lived. Farther south, ice stretched from one side of the horizon to the other. Shackleton calculated that it was "young" ice, and would be easy to break through. He ordered Captain Worsley to carve a passage by ramming forward at top speed. But progress was slow, and again the ice refroze behind the ship as quickly as it passed through. On January 16, seals surfaced from under the ice and vanished northward, as if they knew the Antarctic winter had arrived much earlier than expected.

By January 19, 1915, the *Endurance* was clamped in a vise of solid ice. It was summertime; the seas should have been open. But the ship was held fast. There was no way to escape.

SHACKLETON'S UNEXPECTED RIVAL

Raising funds for another Antarctic expedition was complicated by a rival that Shackleton had never dealt with before— war. On July 28, 1914, as Shackleton was soliciting money for a new foray to the South Pole, Archduke Francis Ferdinand of Austria and his wife were assassinated by a Serbian patriot as they traveled through Sarajevo, Bosnia. Austria immediately declared war on Serbia. By July 30, Russia had mobilized its troops, prompting Germany to declare war against Russia on August 1. Two days later, Germany also declared war against France; then on August 4, England declared war against Germany. In less than a week, Europe was plunged headlong into the First World War. America remained neutral until 1917, then also entered the fray. With Englishmen dying in foreign lands, an Antarctic exploration was of little interest to most Britons. Shackleton's efforts to raise money for a new expedition was therefore difficult, and even aroused a certain scorn among his countrymen.

Shackleton was determined not to let his men see how concerned he was. During the first week of February, a fierce storm seemed to open a path for the *Endurance*, yet no sooner had her engines begun to turn than ice slammed into her, clamping her tight again. March came—the beginning of true winter. For nine months, the ice drifted with the ocean's current, carrying the *Endurance* with it as if she were a kidnapped bride, her masts shrouded in white.

It was important to keep the men busy, so Shackleton sent them onto the ice to build huts and hunt seals. The dogs were exercised to keep them in shape. When spring came, Shackleton assured his men, the situation would improve. He repeated the same words like a mantra: *when spring comes, when spring comes . . .*

All through August, the ship was held fast. September arrived, with no relief. On October 15, the *Endurance* was released briefly, only to be imprisoned again. The future looked bleak. The sides of the ship

Frank Wild, the ENDURANCE'S second in command, skinning a seal for supper, with Shackleton at Patience Camp. They, along with the rest of the ship's crew, drifted on an ice floe for 165 days after the ENDURANCE went down in the Weddell Sea.

had been punctured by huge daggers of ice, and her beams began to snap like matchsticks.

About five o'clock in the afternoon on October 27, 1915, the *Endurance* was abandoned. Three lifeboats—the *James Caird*, the *Stancomb Wills*, and the *Dudley Docker*—along with dogs, supplies, tents, and as much equipment as could be carried off the ship were unloaded onto the ice. As the men worked feverishly, the groans of the dying vessel sounded like the "cries of a living creature."

When they gathered to watch the *Endurance* in her death throes, Captain Worsley remarked, "We had been cast out into a white wilder-

The doomed ENDURANCE, as she began to sink under the ice of the Weddell Sea in October 1915.

ness." As always, Shackleton consoled his men. As soon as the weather warmed, he said, they would put to sea in the smaller boats, and head for one of the Norwegian whaling ports in the area.

No sooner had camp been made on an ice floe and the men settled themselves for sleep the first night, then the floe started to break up. Another frantic move had to be made in pitch darkness, as the camp transferred to a larger floe 200 yards (183 meters) away. At dawn, Shackleton gathered the crew together and told them they would have to begin manhauling the three small boats over the ice in the direction of the Palmer Peninsula, 350 miles (563 kilometers) distant, where open water was certain to be found.

The Antarctic ice wasn't a solid, silent enemy. It shifted constantly, grinding against itself and pitching twenty-ton ice boulders into the air with explosive force. The racket sounded like cannon fire, straining everyone's nerves, though Shackleton seldom showed that it weighed on his.

On the evening of November 21, 1915, Shackleton and his men turned back to see the *Endurance* slip completely under the ice, which slammed over her like the lid on a coffin. "Ship and store have gone," Shackleton announced calmly, "so now we'll go home."

Home! No word could have sounded warmer or more comforting. Neither Shackleton nor his crew could imagine the long and terrible ordeal they would face before they laid eyes on England again.

SEVEN

He Never Spares Himself

On the morning of April 9, 1916—more than a year after the *Endurance* was trapped in the ice, having been carried more than 2,000 miles (3,218 kilometers) across the ocean—an opening finally appeared in the pack ice. Shackleton ordered the three lifeboats into the roiling sea. He set off first, in the largest one, the *James Caird*, with ten crewmen, including Frank Wild. The two smaller craft followed. Soon, the boats were sheeted in ice, yet Shackleton's craggy face betrayed none of his own uncertainty.

Dodging the huge chunks of ice was a harrowing job, but Shackleton knew that such small boats would be smashed like eggshells if they were caught between the edges of those massive cakes. He was determined to save his men and himself, no matter what it took. "He never spares himself, if . . . he can benefit anyone else," Thomas Orde-Lees, a crew member noted in his diary.

On the first night, the crew camped on an ice floe, but it began to break apart near midnight. One of the men, trapped inside his sleeping bag, was dumped through a four-foot-wide crack into the freezing ocean. He was hauled to safety seconds before the split in the ice slammed shut again, which would have crushed him to death.

After the rescue, Shackleton lit a small alcohol stove, heated water mixed with dried milk, and gathered the men around him to sip something warm for courage. Even under such arduous conditions, "Shackleton had that personality that imbued you with trust—you felt that if he led you everything was going to be all right," one man remembered.

Constant rowing through rough seas while crouched on the hard seats of the lifeboats caused saltwater boils to erupt on the men's buttocks. Fatigue made them delirious. Thoughts of food tormented them. Worst of all, terrible thirst plagued them night and day.

On April 14, 1916, Elephant Island—a rocky outcropping about 23 miles (37 kilometers) long and 13 miles (21 kilometers) wide, named for the elephant seals that once congregated on its beaches—was sighted. The stone cliffs that rose above the jagged shoreline made a landing hazardous, but on the morning of April 15, the three boats were put safely ashore.

It was the first time human beings had set foot on the island since American sealers landed there in 1821. The twenty-eight men in Shackleton's expedition were frostbitten, starving, and half-crazed from their terrible ordeal. But they were alive, and that was what mattered to their leader. For months, the men had dreamed of fresh water, and a glacier-water spring bubbled up through the rocks at the edge of Elephant Island. They drank greedily, then staggered drunkenly around the beach as if the water were whiskey. It was the first time they'd stood on solid ground since December 5, 1914, sixteen months earlier.

Their delight with the small beach was short-lived, because tidemarks indicated that it was constantly washed by water. The following

Captain Frank Worsley, without whose excellent navigational skills the lifeboats—the JAMES CAIRD, the DUDLEY DOCKER, and the STANCOMB WILLS—could not have made the voyage through choppy seas from Patience Camp to the safety of Elephant Island, nor from there to the island of South Georgia.

Left Behind

The twenty-two men who were left behind on Elephant Island built themselves an 18 by 10 foot (5.5 by 3 kilometer) hut. They overturned the *Dudley Docker* and the *Stancomb Wills* to make its roof. Rock walls were constructed for the sides, and the whole affair was covered with the tattered remains of their canvas tents. The hut wasn't high enough for a man to stand up in; the roof leaked; snow blew through cracks in the rock walls. Unwittingly, they had picked a spot that had been a penguin rookery, and they discovered too late that the stench created by decades of bird droppings was overwhelming. Even so, when a young member of the expedition named Blackborrow needed surgery to remove all five frostbitten toes on his left foot, he came out of the anesthetic "as cheerful as anything," his companions said.

day, the three small boats were put back into the sea and a permanent camp was made at a better location, 7 miles (11.3 kilometers) to the west.

However, Shackleton realized that no one would ever look for the survivors of the *Endurance* on such an insignificant speck of rock. Unfortunately, South Georgia, and the safety of the whaling station, was still 700 miles (1,126 kilometers) away. Worst of all, most of the members of the crew were far too exhausted to set out on such a long voyage. Shackleton's profound sense of responsibility for his men's welfare left him but one choice—he would set out for South Georgia himself.

On April 19, Shackleton asked for five volunteers to accompany him in the *James Caird*. The lifeboat—only 22 feet (6.7 meters) long, with a beam of 6.5 feet (2 meters) —was hardly the kind of vessel to undertake such a voyage in hostile seas. Nevertheless, just past noon on Monday, April 24, 1916, with Shackleton and five others, the *James Caird* was put back into the water.

Shackleton, a weary man of forty-two years, knew that the fate of everyone—those sailing with him in the *James Caird*, as well as those left behind on Elephant Island—depended on his judgment. On their first night at sea, he ordered four of the men to crawl under the canvas cover of the *James Caird* to rest, while he kept watch with Captain Worsley. Overhead, the Southern Cross glittered cold and clear in the black Antarctic sky, and Worsley later recalled that Shackleton talked till dawn. At six o'clock in the morning, as the sky lightened, Worsley yawned, and Shackleton told him to sleep while he stayed at the tiller.

The *James Caird* made 45 miles (72.4 kilometers) on its first day out. Then the seas switched, becoming cross seas that ran west-south-west, and the wind picked up. Four of the men—Shackleton among them—became violently seasick from the constant heaving and pitching of the tiny vessel. Yet every now and then penguins were seen, and an albatross that had followed the boat since its departure from Elephant Island maintained a steady vigil overhead.

The whole world was gray—gray sky, gray water—and the days merged with one another. The men were constantly water-soaked; their faces and hands were blistered by salt spray. By April 29, Worsley calculated they'd come about 238 miles (383 kilometers); land was still a seemingly impossible 462 miles (743 kilometers) away.

On April 24, 1916, Shackleton and a crew of five left Elephant Island in the JAMES CAIRD, and set out for the Norwegian whaling station, Grytviken, on the island of South Georgia, 700 miles away. The voyage took seventeen days, and the 22-foot (6.7 meter) boat was nearly capsized by huge waves.

On May 5, twelve days after the departure from Elephant Island, Shackleton's spirits were lifted when he saw what he believed was a streak of clear sky on the south-southwest horizon. Thank God, he thought; fairer weather was at hand. Seconds later, he realized with horror that what he'd seen was a monstrously huge wave.

"For God's sake, hold on!" he cried. "It's got us." The *James Caird*—which had lost its sea anchor—was hurled skyward like a cork. The men bailed frantically and prayed hard. Twenty minutes later, the near-fatal crisis had passed, and the six men were grateful to find themselves still alive.

On a foggy May 8, after fifteen days at sea, small birds were seen hovering in the air. Seaweed floated past. Larger birds soon appeared. Worsley estimated they were within 15 miles (24 kilometers) of South Georgia. When the fog lifted, a rocky crag was sighted, vanished in the mist, then reappeared.

The only landing site to be found was in King Haakon Bay, one of the most dangerous locations on the coast of South Georgia. It took two days of fighting wind and waves for the crew to be able to pull the *James Caird* safely onto the beach. On Wednesday, May 10, 1916, seventeen days after leaving Elephant Island, the six men crawled under a notch in the cliff to rest. Five days later, the camp was moved to a more sheltered cove that had a good supply of driftwood for fires. As had been done back at Elephant Island, the *Caird* was turned upside down, and walls of rock, moss, and tussock grass were built around it. The *James Caird*'s sail served as a door. The place was christened Peggoty Camp, after the boathouse in Dickens' novel, *David Copperfield*.

It was true that the men had reached the longed-for destination of South Georgia, but the whaling camp was on the far side of the island. Shackleton knew that he dared not take time to rest and that a journey overland must begin as quickly as possible.

Friday night, May 19, was moonlit. At two o'clock in the morning, Shackleton, Worsley, and Crean set off. From sea level, they climbed 2,500 feet (762 meters) up a steep outcropping of rock, only to discover that the way forward was blocked. They backtracked and started over. At every step, they sank to their knees in snow that was soft and mushy. By noon, they reached the crest, but what they saw was discouraging: A field of broken ice stretched before them that would take days or weeks to traverse. Again they were forced to backtrack and seek a safer descent down the opposite side to the coast.

When a better route was found, Shackleton decided that proceeding step-by-step down the slope would take too long. Why not slide down? Each man carried a coil of rope with him, which he sat on, using it like a saucer-sled, and flew down the opposite side of the 1,500 foot (457 meter) glacier in three minutes.

Even so, they were still not quite halfway to their destination. All three men were exhausted. Haste was important, but Shackleton knew that rest was essential, too. They curled up together, like sledge dogs in the snow, to nap for a few minutes. Then, as Crean made breakfast, Shackleton heard what sounded like a whistle. It was the steam whistle that called the men to work at the whaling station, miles away!

"Never had any of us heard sweeter music," he admitted later. It was the first indication of human life other than their own that any of them had heard since leaving Grytviken in December 1914.

EIGHT

A Lone Star above the Bay

On Saturday afternoon, May 20, 1916, Shackleton, Worsley, and Crean staggered into the whaling station. Except for a quick nap in the snow, they had traveled without pause for thirty-six hours. Matthias Andersen, the English-speaking Norwegian station foreman, stared in amazement at the three men who stood before him. They hadn't changed their clothes in six months, and they were filthy and ragged, their eyes red-rimmed with exhaustion. In a cracked, broken voice, Shackleton asked to speak to the station manager.

The station manager, Captain Thoralf Sorlle arranged for hot baths, clean clothing, and food for the trio. Next he ordered that the *Samson*, a whaler, be sent to rescue the three men who'd been left at King Haakon Bay, on the far side of the island. The *James Caird* was brought back, too, and Captain Worsley remembered that every man at the station wanted a hand in hauling the gallant little

Twenty-two men had been left behind on Elephant Island, and Shackleton returned to rescue them on August 30, 1916. Britain was slow in responding to his plea for help, so Shackleton borrowed the ship YELCHO from the Chilean navy to pick up his men.

boat onto the wharf. "Congratulations from them meant something," Worsley said.

As for crossing South Georgia safely, Shackleton didn't take credit himself for it. "I have no doubt that Providence guided us," he wrote.

But the adventure wasn't over yet; there were twenty-two men seven hundred miles away on Elephant Island who had to be rescued. Shackleton knew they'd be nearly out of food and close to starvation; as when he had decided to cross the island of South Georgia, he knew there was no time to waste. Three days after his arrival at Grytviken, a whaler, the *Southern Sky*, was sent out, only to be forced back by bad weather and pack ice. Another attempt was made on May 26, and another on May 28, both without success.

On May 31, Shackleton desperately cabled King Edward and the admiralty in London, requesting the immediate dispatch of either the *Discovery*, Robert F. Scott's old ship, or a seagoing icebreaker. Britain was consumed by war, however, and a reply was slow in coming.

Nevertheless, the *Daily Chronicle* announced the amazing news of the survival of the *Endurance* expedition on its front page: SAFE ARRIVAL OF SIR ERNEST SHACKLETON AT FALKLAND ISLANDS.

But Shackleton had enemies, and some weren't shy about stating their opinions. He was criticized for having pursued his Antarctic explorations during wartime, while other men were dying in battle. His choice was viewed as self-serving, and a Scottish newspaper, the *Strathspey Herald*, minced no words in an editorial: "We have little use for Sir E. Shackleton."

Finally, the Chilean government offered one of its vessels, the *Yelcho*, for the Elephant Island rescue. On Wednesday, August 30, 1916, more than four months after Shackleton set off in the *James Caird*, while the survivors drank a thin stew made of old seal bones in their hut, one of them noticed a curious-looking piece of ice on the horizon.

Minutes later, the men realized it was a ship. They watched as it came within 150 yards (137 meters) of shore, and a lifeboat was lowered. The men recognized Shackleton at its bow. "I felt jolly near blubbering," Wild confessed. The man to whom they'd entrusted their lives hadn't failed them. Gratitude went both ways. Worsley remembered the "years literally seemed to drop" from Shackleton when he counted the figures on shore: Every single man had survived!

It gave Shackleton satisfaction to rescue his men himself, without the help of the British navy. He couldn't understand the attitude of officials in his own country, but he left no doubt how he felt when he wrote to Emily. "Damn the Admiralty," he stormed. For the crew of the *Endurance*, however, he had only praise. "No words can do justice to their courage . . . To walk beside death for months . . . that's the spirit that makes courage worth having."

Before returning to England, Shackleton lectured in New Zealand and Australia, and in U.S. cities such as San Francisco, Portland, Seattle, Chicago, and New York, where he spoke at Carnegie Hall on April 29, 1917. When he reached home in May, he found Britain a different nation from the one he'd left in 1914. It had been changed forever by the horrors of World War I; nations had been torn apart, and great loss of life had been endured. By comparison, polar exploration seemed a trivial personal indulgence.

British men aged seventeen to forty-one years of age were being drafted for military service, but Shackleton, age forty-three, was exempt. Nevertheless, he was eager to do something for his country, and traveled to South America to bolster support for the British cause, then organized the transportation of men and equipment to Russia to help the war effort.

Even so, Emily wrote to a friend that her husband was "restless— & is chafing to be off." Many of his old debts still hadn't been paid, and his aged parents needed financial help. His own children would have welcome his companionship, yet in the back of Shackleton's mind lingered the dream of returning one more time to Antarctica and achieving the kind of towering greatness that had so far eluded him.

"I am mad to get away," he admitted to a friend, and lamented how "the years are piling up." Old friends noticed with regret that he smoked and drank heavily and had aged dramatically.

In 1920, with financial backing from a Dulwich classmate and help from his old friend, Hugh Robert Mill, Shackleton launched what he named the British Oceanographical and Sub-Antarctic Expedition. Its purpose would be to circumnavigate the Antarctic, map its coastline, explore the islands in the area, and do additional research in meteorology and marine biology. The expedition, which had eighteen members—including six from the *Endurance* voyage (who had not yet been paid in full)—left England on September 17 aboard the *Quest*. What had started as an adventure in his youth had for Shackleton become an obsession as he grew older. His former crewmates noticed the change. "There is something different about him this trip as compared with the last, which I do not understand," said one.

Then, while en route to the Antarctic for the fourth time, Shackleton suffered a heart attack. As always, he refused to be treated for it, yet he admitted in his diary, "I grow old and tired, but must always lead on." The truth was, Ernest Shackleton couldn't *not* return to the Antarctic. It was there, surrounded by frozen beauty and arduous challenges, that Shackleton felt most at home.

On January 4, 1922, the *Quest* arrived in Grytviken, filling Shackleton with warm memories of the past. A new year was beginning; the future held the promise of success. That evening, "in the darkening twilight," Shackleton wrote in his diary, he saw "a lone star hover, gemlike above the bay."

The vision of that star at the southernmost tip of the world was his last. In the early hours of January 5, 1922, Ernest Shackleton died of a final heart attack. Years before, he had confided to an admirer that he didn't want to die in England. Fate granted his wish.

Shackleton's body was to be taken to England for burial, but his wife requested that it be buried at South Georgia. On March 5, 1922, he was laid to rest in the barren, windswept Norwegian cemetery for whalers at Grytviken. No one knew better than Emily Shackleton that it was where her husband truly belonged.

In 1932, ten years after his death, the Royal Geographical Society erected a statue honoring Shackleton at its London headquarters. It is ironic that even though he never planted the British flag at the Pole as he so desired, never traversed Antarctica as he'd planned, didn't circumnavigate the continent as he'd dreamed, Shackleton came to be one of the most widely admired of all polar explorers. Roald Amundsen expressed

Shackleton died at South Georgia, January 5, 1922, at the age of forty-seven, on his fourth and final voyage to Antarctica. His wife requested that he be laid to rest in the windswept Norwegian Whalers' cemetery at Grytviken in the frozen land he loved so well.

---

it best in a letter to the London *Daily Chronicle* on February 23, 1917:

> *"Do not let it be said that Shackleton failed . . . No man fails who sets an example of high courage, of unbroken resolution, of unshrinking endurance."*

It was Shackleton's ability to lead men, to inspire them to live beyond themselves, that set him apart. Perhaps his finest legacy is that to the end of his life, Ernest Shackleton lived up to his family's motto: "By endurance we conquer."

Aftermath

In 1950, the American geophysicist, Dr. James Van Allen met with other scientists at his home in Maryland. Out of their discussions came the International Geophysical Year—the IGY. It involved more than 30,000 scientists from around the world. Their objective was to study meteorology, glaciology, magnetism, seismology, volcanism, oceanography, and all aspects of life at the bottom of the world. Even more importantly, they pledged to share the information that had been collected.

In 1959, twelve nations—Argentina, Australia, Belgium, Chile, France, Japan, New Zealand, Norway, South Africa, the Soviet Union, the United Kingdom, and the U.S.—signed the Antarctic Treaty in Washington, D.C. The signers of the treaty pledged that Antarctica shall "be used for peaceful purposes only. There shall be prohibited . . . any measures of a military nature."

Aftermath

Today, the activity in the Antarctic is scientific in nature. Even as the century turns, it is still a place where men—and women—can choose to test their mettle against the elements that dealt so harshly with Shackleton and Scott. In 1994, Liv Arneson, a schoolteacher from Norway, skied solo to the South Pole. In 2000, Arneson was joined by Ann Bancroft, a physical education instructor from Minnesota, and the two women crossed the continent of Antarctica.

Sir Ernest Shackleton and His Times

1847   Ernest Shackleton is born in Kilkea, Ireland.

1902   Robert F. Scott, Edward Wilson, and Ernest Shackleton leave base camp at McMurdo Sound and reach 82° South latitude, 400 miles (644 kilometers) from the South Pole, before they are forced back.

1908   Ernest Shackleton, with three companions, comes within 112 miles (180 kilometers) of the South Pole, besting Scott's record.

1911   Roald Amundsen of Norway, with four companions, reaches the South Pole on December 14.

1912   Robert F. Scott, with five companions, reaches the South Pole in January, to find the Norwegian flag planted there; all the men perish on the return to base camp.

1915   Ernest Shackleton's ship, the *Endurance*, with a crew of twenty-eight, is crushed by ice in the Weddell Sea; the crew takes refuge on Elephant Island.

1916   Shackleton, with five men, heads for South Georgia in a lifeboat; the men on Elephant Island are rescued later.

1922   Shackleton, on his fourth trip to the Antarctic, dies of a heart attack at South Georgia; he is buried in Norwegian whalers' cemetery.

FURTHER RESEARCH

Books

Armstrong, Jennifer. *Shipwreck at the Bottom of the World: The Extraordinary True Story of Shackleton and the* Endurance. New York: Crown, 1998.

Crossly, Louise. *Explore Antarctica.* New York: Cambridge University Press, 1995.

Johnson, Rebecca L. *Braving the Frozen Frontier: Women Working in Antarctica.* Minneapolis: Lerner Publications, 1997.

Kimmel, Elizabeth Cody. *Ice Story: Shackleton's Lost Expedition.* New York: Clarion Books, 1999.

Kostyal, K.M. *Trial by Ice: A Photobiography of Sir Ernest Shackleton.* Washington, D.C.: National Geographic Society, 1999.

McCurdy, Michael. *Trapped by the Ice! Shackleton's Amazing Antarctic Adventure.* New York: Walker and Company, 1997.

Websites

An Antarctic Time Line: 1519–1959
www.south-pole.com/p0000052.htm

The ENDURANCE
www.kodak.com/US/en/corp/features/endurance

Shackleton's Legendary Antarctic Expedition
www.amnh.org/exhibitions/shackleton

Bibliography

Alexander, Caroline. *The* Endurance: *Shackleton's Legendary Antarctic Expedition.* New York: Alfred A. Knopf, 1999.

Amundsen, Roald. *The South Pole: An Account of the Norwegian Antarctic Expedition in the Fram, 1910–1912.* New York: Cooper Square Press, 2001.

Bickel, Lennard. *Shackleton's Forgotten Men: The Untold Tragedy of the* Endurance *Epic.* New York: Thunder's Mouth Press, 2000.

Bryce, Robert M. *Cook and Peary: The Polar Controversy, Resolved.* Mechanicsburg, PA: Stackpole Books, 1999.

Caras, Roger. *Antarctica: Land of Frozen Time.* Philadelphia: Chilton Books, 1962.

Carr, Tim and Pauline Carr. *Antarctic Oasis: Under the Spell of South Georgia.* New York, W. W. Norton & Company, 1998.

Gurney, Alan. *Below the* Convergence: *Voyages Toward Antarctica, 1699–1839.* New York: W. W. Norton & Company, 1997.

Huntford, Roland. *Shackleton.* New York: Atheneum, 1986.

Huxley, Elspeth. *Scott of the Antarctic.* New York: Atheneum, 1978.

May, John. *The Greenpeace Book of Antarctica: A New View of the Seventh Continent.* New York: Doubleday, 1989.

Mear, Roger and Robert Swan. *A Walk to the Pole: To the Heart of Antarctica in the Footsteps of Scott.* New York: Crown, 1987.

Nordenskjold, Otto. *Antarctic, Vol 1.* Stockholm: Bonniers Forlag, 1904.

Preston, Diana. *A First Rate Tragedy: Robert Falcon Scott and the Race to the South Pole.* Boston: Houghton Mifflin Company, 1998.

Scott, Robert Falcon. *The Voyage of the* Discovery, *2 Vols.* London: Smith Elder & Co., 1905.

Shackleton, Ernest. *Shackleton, His Antarctic Writings.* London: British Broadcasting Corp., 1983.

Bibliography

Shackleton, Ernest. *The Heart of the Antarctic: Being the Story of the British Antarctic Expedition 1907–1909. Vol. 1 & Vol. 2.* Philadelphia: J. B. Lippincott Company, 1909.

Shackleton, Ernest. *South: The Story of Shackleton's Last Expedition, 1914–17.* North Pomfret, VT: Trafalgar Square Publishing, 1999.

Worsley, Frank A. *Shackleton's Boat Journey.* New York: W. W. Norton & Company, 1977.

Worsley, Frank A. Endurance: *An Epic of Polar Adventure.* New York: W. W. Norton & Company, 1999.

Source Notes

Foreword:

P. 5: "I think this Southern land…": Roger Caras, *Antarctica: Land of Frozen Time* (Chilton Books, 1962), p. 16.

Chapter 1:

p. 8: "a Viking with a mother's heart": Margot Morrell, Stephanie Capparell, *Shackleton's Way: Leadership Lessons from the Great Antarctic Explorer* Viking, 2001), p. 18.

p. 8: "always friendly and good natured": Roland Huntford, *Shackleton* (Atheneum, 1986), p. 7.

p. 8: "odd boy who, in spite of an adventurous nature…" K. M. Kostyal, *Trial by Ice* (National Geographic Society, 1999), p. 10.

p. 8: "We never discovered you when you were at Dulwich…": Morrell, p. 20.

p. 9: "stab another with a knife…": Huntford, p. 15.

p. 9: "The first night I took out my Bible…": Margery Fisher, James Fisher, *Shackleton and the Antarctic* (Houghton Mifflin Company, 1958), p. 7.

p. 9: "it is pretty hard work": Huntford, p. 13.

p.10: "Strangely drawn towards the mysterious south": Huntford, p.24.

p. 10: "Old Shacks…busy with his books": Huntford, p. 17.

p. 10: "For all is new…": H. G. R. King, *The Antarctic* (Arco Publishing, 1969), p. 10.

p. 10: "strangely drawn towards the mysterious south": Huntford, p. 24.

p. 10: "the most pig-headed, obstinate boy…": Fisher & Fisher, p. 8.

Chapter 2:

p. 13: "Is the last great piece of maritime exploration…": Fisher & Fisher, p. 17.

P. 13: "I have…position and money": Fisher & Fisher, p. 22.

P. 15: "youth is essential…": Huntford, p. 27.

p. 16: "fortunate in finding such an excellent…": Huntford, p. 34.

p. 17: "consent to your union…": Huntford, p. 44.

p. 17: "inexhaustible good humor…": Fisher & Fisher, p. 26.

p. 17: "was always ready to have yarn with us…": Fisher & Fisher, p. 46.

p. 22: "the best qualities of all the penny and halfpenny London dailies…": Fisher & Fisher, p. 41.

p. 22: "striking personality, admirable humour, and inexhaustible energy…": Fisher & Fisher, p. 50.

Chapter 3

p. 23: "danger is rife…we did not expect a feather bed…": Fisher & Fisher, p. 57.

p. 26: "a small sanctuary for happy recollections": Fisher & Fisher, p. 58.

p. 26: "the absolutely unknown South…": Fisher & Fisher, p. 58.

p. 26: "I believe in God…": Fisher & Fisher, p. 59.

p. 26: "we had immense help from our dogs…": Otto Nodenskjold, *Antarctic*, *Vol. 1* (Bonniers Forlag, 1904), p. 327.

p. 28: "Medical exmtn. Shews Captain [Scott] and I to be inclined to scurvy…": Fisher & Fisher, pp. 61–62.

p. 28: "Clarence gave up the ghost…": Fisher & Fisher, p. 66.

p. 29: "swollen lips & peeled complexion…": Huntford, p. 113.

p. 29: "wasn't up to the mark…": Huntford, p. 113.

p. 29: "but a sad one indeed for me…": Fisher & Fisher, p. 76.

Chapter 4:

p. 31: "There was something about him that compelled confidence…": Fisher & Fisher, p. 81.

p. 33: "It will be a great thing for the Society…": Huntford, p. 135.

p. 33–34: "had a true sailor's love for spinning a yarn…": F. W. Everett, *Royal Magazine*, June 1902, p. 192.

p.34: "an unprincipled attempt . . .": Bryce, p. 210.

p. 34: "Our invalid was so exhausted…": Robert F. Scott, *The Voyage of the* Discovery, *2 Vols.* (Smith Elder & Co., 1905), p. 90.

p. 35: "I got all the applause…": Huntford, p. 148.

p. 35: "One must not chain down an eagle in a barnyard…": Huntford, p. 121.

p. 36: "Don't say No until we have had a talk…" Huntford, p. 159.

Chapter 5:

p. 37: "I do wholly agree with the right lying with Scott…": Huntford, p. 162.

p. 38: "I think he examined the specialist…": Huntford,   p. 167.

p. 39: "too little time…": Huntford, p. 170.

p. 40: "There was about him the unmistakable look of a deep-sea sailor…": Huntford, p. 176.

p. 40: "The presence of the dogs…": Ernest Shackleton, *The Heart of the Antarctic* (J. B. Lippincott Company, 1909), p. 138.

p. 41: "A glorious day for our start…": Shackleton, p. 256.

p. 42: "The killing of the ponies…": Shackleton, p. 286.

p. 42–43: "done more than anyone could have believed…": Fisher & Fisher, pp. 227–228.

p. 43: "thin and worn . . .": Fisher & Fisher, p. 228.

p. 44: "far more than his share…": Fisher & Fisher, p. 222.

p. 45: "It's an old dog for the hard road…": Morrell and Capparell, p. 38.

Chapter 6:

p. 46: "a professed liar…": Huntford, p. 304.

p. 48: "acute rheumatism…": Huntford, p. 340.

Source Notes

p. 48: "unless I can be the first to get there…": Huntford, p. 297.

p. 54: "cries of a living creature…": Huntford, p. 454.

p. 54–55: "We had been cast out into a white wilderness…": Marvin H. Albert, *The Long White Road: Ernest Shackleton's Antarctic Adventures* (David McKay Co., Inc., 1957), p. 120.

p. 55: "Ship and stores have gone…": Morell & Capparell, p. 145.

Chapter 7:

p. 56: "He never spares himself…": Huntford, p. 511.

p. 57: "Shackleton had that personality that imbued you with trust…": Huntford, p. 508.

p. 61: "For God's sake, hold on!": Huntford, p. 560.

p. 63: "Never had any of us heard sweeter music…": Huntford, p. 593.

Chapter 8:

p. 65: "Congratulations from them meant something…": Frank A. Worsley, *Endurance: An Epic of Polar Adventure* (W. W. Norton & Company, 1999), p. 165.

p. 65: "I have no doubt that Providence guided us…": Huntford, p. 695.

p. 66: "We have very little use for Sir E. Shackleton…": Editorial, *Strathspey Herald*, June 29, 1916.

p. 66: "I felt jolly near blubbering…": Huntford, p. 621.

p. 66: "years literally seemed to drop…": Worsley, p. 179.

p. 66: "Damn the Admiralty…": Huntford, p. 625.

p. 66–67: "No words can do justice to their courage…": Morrell and Capparrel, p. 198.

p. 67: "restless—& is chafing to be off…": Huntford, p. 651.

p. 67: "I am mad to get away…": Huntford, p. 685.

p. 68: "I grow old and tired…": Morrell & Capparrel, p. 208.

p. 68: "in the darkening twilight…": Huntford, p. 689.

p. 69: "Do not let it be said that Shackleton failed…": Huntford, p. 674.

Index

Page numbers in **boldface** are illustrations.